OIL RIG WORKERS
IN ACTION

BY TYLER OMOTH

The Child's World®
childsworld.com

Published by The Child's World®
1980 Lookout Drive • Mankato, MN 56003-1705
800-599-READ • www.childsworld.com

Photographs ©: iStockphoto, cover, 1; Shutterstock Images, 5, 8, 20, 22, 24; Bradford Martin/iStockphoto, 6; U.S. Coast Guard Atlantic Area, 10; Petty Officer 3rd Class Tom Atkeson/U.S. Coast Guard Atlantic Area, 11; Cheryl Casey/Shutterstock Images, 12; WTM/Shutterstock Images, 14; Borowski/SIPA/Newscom, 17; D. Record/Daily Mirror Mirrorpix/Newscom, 19; Stocktrek Images/Thinkstock, 26; PA Images/Alamy, 28

ISBN 9781503816312

LCCN 2016945626

Printed in the United States of America
PA02320

TABLE OF
CONTENTS

FAST FACTS

What's the Job?

- Offshore oil rigs are platforms that stay out in the ocean.
- Employees work exhausting 12- to 14-hour shifts on the rigs for two weeks at a time.
- Some workers run the large equipment such as drills and cranes. Other workers monitor computer programs.
- Workers are constantly repairing and cleaning equipment on the rig.

The Dangers

- Oil rigs are battered by waves and cold winds.
- Large cranes and drills are constantly in use. Workers can get caught in the machines or hit by moving parts.
- The oil and gases that these rigs collect can burst into flame very easily.
- Accidents can happen when workers are going to and from the rig.

Important Stats

- In 2016, there were 241 offshore oil rigs in the United States alone. Most of them are in the Gulf of Mexico.

- A worker in the oil and gas industry is seven times more likely to be killed on the job than a worker in an average occupation in the United States.

Chapter 1

DISASTER IN THE GULF

Oleander Benton was enjoying life on an offshore oil rig. Offshore oil rigs are large platforms that either float in the water or are secured to the sea floor. The platforms hold powerful drills and other machinery. These tools help workers collect oil that is below the ocean. Workers live on the rigs in special housing during their two-week shifts.

Oleander worked as a cook on a rig called *Deepwater Horizon*. This oil rig was in the Gulf of Mexico, nearly 50 miles (80 km) from the Louisiana shore. Oleander knew that an oil rig needs many people to operate well. Every day, she saw the crew that worked with the giant oil drills. She saw the crane operators who worked on the deck loading and off-loading supplies. She also saw painters, mechanics, and many other workers.

The oil rig offered relatively comfortable living. More than 100 people lived on the rig at any given time. The rig had a movie theater, a gym, and other things that a small town might have.

◀ **The *Deepwater Horizon* was built from December 1998 to February 2001.**

But Oleander was aware that living on an oil rig meant there was always a chance of danger.

On April 20, 2010, Oleander was in the laundry room with a friend. It was Oleander's 52nd birthday. Suddenly, she got a surprise she didn't expect.

A loud boom shook the laundry room. Oleander remembered her training and immediately fell to the floor. She knew the boom was an explosion. On an oil rig far out to sea, an explosion can mean disaster for everyone.

Light fixtures fell from the ceiling and hit her on the head and back. Other fixtures crashed around her. Then she heard her friend screaming in pain. The explosion had blown the heavy door off its hinges. Oleander's friend was pinned to the floor under the door.

Oleander tried to lift the door, but it was too heavy. Her head and back hurt from the **debris** that had fallen on her. She helped her friend slide out from under the door. Then she grabbed her friend's hand as they ran down a dark hallway.

In the chaos, Oleander saw someone calling to them. The people on the rig were used to little things going wrong and being fixed. But this man was waving at them in a panic.

◀ **A wide variety of workers live on oil rigs.**

▲ Boats spray water on the *Deepwater Horizon* in an attempt to stop the flames.

Oleander and her friend knew they needed to **evacuate**. This was no minor emergency. This was a disaster.

They rushed through the maze of broken doors, injured people, and clutter. They were trying to reach the surface of the oil rig. Emergency alarms blasted in their ears. The pair also heard the screams of other injured people.

As they ran, they looked for lighted exit signs. These signs would help them find their way to the top of the rig. Scared, but not seriously injured, the women made it up to the surface.

What they saw when they got there was a horrifying scene. Mud and fire were blasting out of the oil rig's **derrick**.

Oleander stumbled on her way to a lifeboat, but she recovered quickly. Others were not so lucky. All around her, she saw people who were wounded. Some were dead.

Finally, Oleander made her way into the lifeboat. She gave her name to a worker who was creating a list of those who were heading to safety.

▲ Rescue workers assist victims of the *Deepwater Horizon* explosion.

Oleander was taken to a hospital to treat her wounds. She survived with minor injuries to her neck, back, and head. But the explosion on the *Deepwater Horizon* had been a disaster. Eleven people on the rig were killed that night.

Oleander later learned what had happened. As crews were drilling, gas and other material burst from the sea and caused an explosion. The rig's safety measures should have sealed off the well. The well is the source of the oil, which is very flammable. But the machines could not stop the explosions and leaking oil.

Two days after the disaster, Oleander was watching television. She saw that more explosions had torn apart the empty rig. It toppled into the water. The oil continued to spew from the accident for 87 days. Experts estimated that more than 200 million gallons (757 million L) of **crude oil** spilled into the Gulf of Mexico. Millions of animals died, including birds, fish, and dolphins. The oil spill seriously damaged local fishing operations as well as tourism and other industries.

Experts continue to work on new methods and safety features for offshore oil rigs. They hope to prevent future disasters like the *Deepwater Horizon* spill.

◄ **A worker cleans up a beach that was damaged by the oil spill.**

Chapter 2

JUMP!

Life on an oil rig in the North Sea is a constant battle with the elements. Workers are surrounded by cold, choppy water. The rig is the only thing that keeps workers safe from the harsh environment.

In 1988, Ron Carey was working as a **maintenance** technician on the *Piper Alpha* oil rig. The *Piper Alpha* was the biggest oil and natural gas rig in the United Kingdom. Ron's job was crucial to the safety of everyone on the rig. A rig as large as the *Piper Alpha* is loaded with machines, computers, valves, and rigging.

Each day, Ron went to a team meeting after breakfast. Then he followed a schedule of repairs and tests. Each repair or test would make sure that the equipment was in perfect working order. These jobs had to be coordinated with the operation of the rig. That way, other workers would not have to stop for Ron and his team to do their job.

◄ **Oil rigs are lit up brightly so that people can work even when the sun is down.**

Working on equipment sometimes meant climbing high up on scaffolding or fighting strong ocean winds. Ron kept records of every piece of equipment and when it was repaired. It was also important to tell the other workers which systems were being repaired so they did not use them.

On the night of July 6, something went horribly wrong. Earlier that day, crews had performed routine maintenance on some pipes. But they did not tell the night crews which pipes were in use and which ones were shut down for repair. As a result, the night crew used a pipe that was sealed off for repair. Because the pipe was sealed, the gas meant to flow through it had nowhere to go. And there were no safety measures in place to relieve the pressure in the pipe.

While Ron and many other people were sleeping, natural gas began leaking out of the pipe. The leaking gas **ignited**. Ron was awakened by the sound of a huge explosion. Then he heard another.

He quickly decided to make his way to the lifeboats to evacuate. On his way there, he saw men wearing gas masks. They shook their heads. The explosions had destroyed the lifeboats, they said. The fire from the gas leak continued to burn white hot. The fire got its fuel from the pumping natural gas.

A worker watches as the *Piper Alpha* burns. ▶

Ron knew that no safety features could contain explosions this large. The oil rig was going to be destroyed. And the rig was far from shore. That meant rescue workers wouldn't be able to get there before it blew up. Ron's only chance for survival was in the frigid water below. He started for the ropes that divers used to climb down into the sea.

Another explosion rocked the rig. Fire and smoke surrounded him. Ron realized there was no time to find the ropes. He dived off of the platform. Ron fell 50 feet (15 m) before splashing down into the cold water. Oil coated the top of the water. Heat blasted down from the raging fire above on the rig.

Ron repeatedly ducked his head under the water to keep his exposed skin from burning. Then he saw pieces of the rig falling into the water. He had to duck and swim to avoid the debris.

Ron fought to stay afloat in the North Sea. He could see the effects of the accident. The rig was covered in flames. Everything but the drill derrick was destroyed. All of the decks where Ron and his coworkers had worked and slept were completely gone. The rig was now a giant fire in the middle of the North Sea.

Ron saw more than just debris. He also saw coworkers floating in the water. Some of them were clinging to wreckage, fighting for their lives. Others had lost the battle and were already dead.

The *Piper Alpha* burns in the frigid waters of the North Sea. ▶

Ron was determined to survive for the sake of his family. He swam away from the rig and the fires. He found a person wearing a life jacket. The person was dead. Ron could not bring himself to take the life jacket off of the person's body. But he used the body to keep himself afloat.

Soon, rescue boats arrived. They plucked Ron and the other survivors out of the sea. The surviving oil rig workers were relieved to be alive. But they didn't know just how much damage the accident caused.

Ron later learned that the disaster claimed the lives of 167 workers that night. It was the deadliest oil rig accident in history. Only 61 people survived. Many of them, including Ron, were badly burned or injured. The rig was completely destroyed and continued to burn for three weeks. After studying this disaster, experts developed more than 100 new safety suggestions for oil rigs in the North Sea.

◄ **After the *Piper Alpha* disaster, other North Sea oil rigs such as this one began following new safety guidelines.**

Chapter 3

HELICOPTER DOWN

Paul Sharp enjoyed working on offshore oil rigs. He had a loving family at home. But the men and women he worked with at sea were like a second family to him. They worked closely together on the *Borgsten Dolphin* oil rig. This rig was in the North Sea off the coast of Scotland. Paul worked 12-hour shifts for two weeks at a time.

Paul was a scaffolder. He helped build the structures that allowed maintenance crews to do their jobs high above the platform. Each day, Paul and his team created temporary platforms. Other teams used these platforms while doing maintenance or other projects high up on the rig.

Building scaffolding does not require much classroom education. But it requires serious on-the-job training. Workers have to learn how to create scaffolding strong enough to hold the people working on it while combating the winds and waves.

◀ **Scaffolders wear safety equipment so that they will not get hurt if they slip.**

▲ **A Super Puma helicopter carries workers to their oil rig.**

Most days, Paul's work took him several stories above the deck of the oil rig. A scaffolder cannot be afraid of heights.

One day in August 2013, Paul had just finished two weeks of work. Now, he prepared to go home to his family in England. He made his way to the helicopter pad.

A Super Puma helicopter waited to take him and 17 others back to land. Each person put on an **immersion** suit. These suits were designed to keep the workers alive if they somehow ended up in the cold water of the North Sea.

The Super Puma helicopters had a bad reputation among oil rig workers. Four of the helicopters had been in accidents in the previous five years. But Paul was excited to see his family, and the Super Puma was the fastest way off the rig. That convinced Paul and the others to risk getting on a helicopter they didn't trust.

The passengers boarded the helicopter, wearing their immersion suits. They sat facing each other in narrow seats. Paul knew it would be an uncomfortable trip. The passengers prepared for takeoff. They put on ear defenders to protect their hearing from the noisy vehicle.

Paul fell asleep to the sound of the blades. When he woke up, the pilot told them the helicopter was almost ready to land for a fuel stop. But before they could land, Paul heard a loud noise. It sounded like bones cracking. The helicopter began to move side to side. Paul could feel that they were falling. They were going to crash into the ocean.

The helicopter hit the water hard. The rear windows broke open, and the helicopter's blades snapped. Cold water gushed in through every opening.

Paul had no time to put on the hood of his immersion suit. He took one big breath before the water went over his head. Underneath the water, Paul headed to a window. But it wouldn't open. He hit it once, and then he hit it again. On the third time, the window finally released.

Paul crawled through the open space and swam upward. As soon as he reached the surface, he took a huge breath of fresh air. Then he pushed himself away from the wreckage and inflated his immersion suit.

Then Paul heard a cry for help. He grabbed the injured person, swimming away from the helicopter to safer water. The helicopter's fuel covered the water. The polluted water got into Paul's mouth and made him sick. But he knew he couldn't stop. He kept swimming and towing his injured coworker.

Paul noticed that his immersion suit was filling up with water. A piece of the helicopter blade had ripped it. He wouldn't be able to stay afloat for very long.

Other passengers from the wreck had managed to inflate two life rafts. Paul and the others climbed into the rafts. Once they were safe, they saw that the helicopter had almost reached the shore. A crash on land would have been much more devastating.

◀ **Bright orange immersion suits keep victims warm and make them easy for rescue workers to spot.**

After 30 minutes, the sound of a rescue helicopter rang through the sky. Moments later, they were air-lifted to safety.

Paul lost four of his coworkers that day. Three drowned, and one had a heart attack. Working on an oil rig is dangerous. But getting to and from the rig is the most dangerous part of the job. Paul's calm thinking and quick reactions kept him alive and saved the life of a coworker.

THINK ABOUT IT

- Oil rig workers usually stay on their rig for two weeks at a time. That's 14 days without seeing family or even land. They also work in 12-hour shifts. Would you be able to handle this job? Why or why not?
- The United States uses millions of gallons of oil each day. How would the world be different without oil rig workers?
- There are many jobs on an oil rig. What job would you want? Would you climb high up like the scaffolders? Would you want to run the big machines, such as the cranes?
- How could the oil industry make offshore oil rigs safer?

◄ Wreckage of the Super Puma helicopter floats in the sea.

GLOSSARY

crude oil (KROOD OIL): Crude oil is oil that has not yet been made into products. Crude oil can be made into gasoline, jet fuel, and other products.

debris (duh-BREE): Debris is the pieces of something that has been broken or destroyed. After the explosion on the oil rig, debris fell into the sea.

derrick (DER-ick): A derrick is the tower that holds all of the machines used for drilling oil wells. The derrick on an oil rig is very tall.

evacuate (i-VAK-yoo-ate): Evacuate means to leave an area because there is danger. Workers had to evacuate the oil rig after the explosion.

ignited (ig-NITE-ed): Ignited means caught fire or blew up. After the leaking gas ignited, there was a huge explosion.

immersion (i-MUHR-shuhn): Immersion means something is completely covered by liquid. The workers put on immersion suits so they would not freeze in the ocean.

maintenance (MAYN-tuh-nuhns): Maintenance is the process of keeping things in proper working condition. Workers performed maintenance on the rig to make sure everything ran smoothly.

TO LEARN MORE

Books

Goldsworthy, Steve. *Oil Rig Operator*. New York: AV2 by
　　Weigl, 2014.

Nelson, Drew. *Life on an Oil Rig*. New York: Gareth Stevens
　　Publishing, 2013.

Thomas, William. *Oil Rig Worker*. New York: Marshall
　　Cavendish Benchmark, 2011.

Web Sites

Visit our Web site for links about oil rig workers:
childsworld.com/links

*Note to Parents, Teachers, and Librarians: We routinely verify our Web links to make sure
they are safe and active sites. So encourage your readers to check them out!*

SELECTED BIBLIOGRAPHY

Edemariam, Aida. "Super Puma Helicopter Crash: Survivors
　　on Britain's Toughest Commute." *The Guardian*.
　　Guardian News and Media Limited, 29 Mar. 2014. Web.
　　30 June 2016.

"Gulf Oil Spill Inferno: Witnesses Recount Blast on Doomed
　　Rig." *Cleveland.com*. Advance Ohio, 9 May 2010. Web.
　　30 June 2016.

Macalister, Terry. "Piper Alpha Disaster: How 167 Oil Rig
　　Workers Died." *The Guardian*. Guardian News and Media
　　Limited, 4 July 2013. Web. 30 June 2016.

INDEX

ABOUT THE AUTHOR

Tyler Omoth has written more than 25 books for kids, covering a wide variety of topics. He has also published poetry and award-winning short stories. He loves sports and new adventures. Tyler currently lives in sunny Brandon, Florida, with his wife, Mary.